Integrated **1** Mathematics

Explorations Lab Manual

The Explorations Lab Manual includes additional explorations for use with various sections in the student text and diagram masters, including data sheets, for use with many of the explorations in the student text. Answers to the additional explorations are provided following the diagram masters.

McDougal Littell/Houghton Mifflin

Evanston, Illinois

Boston   Dallas   Phoenix

About the Explorations Lab Manual

The *Explorations Lab Manual* was designed to be used in conjunction with the student textbook. It contains two types of material: **Additional Explorations** and **Diagram Masters.**

Additional Explorations

The Additional Explorations are closely related to the sections in the student textbook. They help you adapt or expand the material in the textbook to the special needs of your classes and your own teaching preferences.

Using Technology For example, if you wish to emphasize the use of calculators or computers, Additional Explorations 4, 5, 7, 8, and 11 will give you additional support in integrating these technologies into your course. On the other hand, for classes that do not have access to graphing technology, Additional Exploration 12 provides a non-technological alternative to the graphics calculator Exploration in the textbook.

Using Manipulatives Many hands-on activities are included in the Explorations in the student textbook. In addition, a number of activities are suggested by the concept developments in the textbook. If you wish to emphasize the use of manipulatives (particularly algebra tiles) in your course, Additional Explorations 1, 2, 3, 6, 9, 10, 13, 14 will help you expand the material presented in the text.

Diagram Masters

The diagram masters were also designed to be used in conjunction with the student textbook. Two types of masters are included: Diagram Masters 1-7 are for general use with the course; Diagram Masters 8-22 are for use with specific Explorations in the textbook. Most of the masters in this second group are data collection sheets to facilitate data collection by students.

ISBN: 0-395-69816-2

23456789 - HS - 98 97 96 95

Contents

Additional Explorations

Diagram Masters

Additional Exploration 1

For use with Section 1-5

How can you use algebra tiles to model
combining like terms?

Materials: *Algebra tiles*

● ●

1. You can use algebra tiles to model variable expressions.
   Use three *x*-tiles and four 1-tiles to model the expression
   $3x + 4$.

2. Below the model for $3x + 4$, make a model for $2x + 3$.

3. Now put the tiles for both expressions together.

   How many *x*-tiles do you have in all? _____

   How many 1-tiles in all? _____

4. What expression do the combined tiles represent?

   _____

5. Look at the model on your table. Complete the following
   statement:

   $(3x + 4) + (2x + 3) =$ _____

6. Clear away the tiles you used in 1–5. You may remember
   that the large square tile is an x^2-tile.

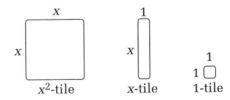

x^2-tile   *x*-tile   1-tile

Use x^2-tiles, *x*-tiles, and 1-tiles to copy the model below.

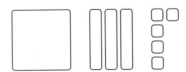

What variable expression does the model represent?

_____

(continued)

Additional Exploration 1 *(continued)*

7. Leave the tiles for step 6 in place. Below them, use tiles to model $2x^2 + x + 3$.

8. Combine the tiles from steps 6 and 7.

   In all, how many x^2-tiles are there? _____

   In all, how many x-tiles are there? _____

   In all, how many 1-tiles are there? _____

9. What expression do the combined tiles represent?

   _____

10. Use steps 6–9 to complete the following statement:

    (_____) + $(2x^2 + x + 3)$ = _____ .

11. Use algebra tiles to model and simplify
    $(3x^2 + 5x + 7) + (4x^2 + 5)$.

Name _____ Date _____

Additional Exploration 2

For use with Section 2-2

This Exploration may be substituted for the Exploration in the text.

How can you use integer chips to model integer operations?

Materials: *Integer chips*

● ●

1. A ☐ chip represents +1, or 1.

   A ▨ chip represents −1.

   What integer does each group of chips represent?

   Notice that since 1 + (−1) = 0, a pair of opposite chips can be grouped to form a **zero pair** whose value is 0.

   _____   _____   _____

2. To model the addition problem 4 + (−8), put down four 1 chips and eight −1 chips. Then remove as many zero pairs as possible.

   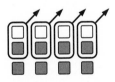

   Complete: Since there are _____ −1 chips left,

   4 + (−8) = _____ .

3. Explain how to use integer chips to represent −2 + 6 and

   then find the sum. _____

   _____

   _____

   _____

(continued)

3

Additional Exploration 2 *(continued)*

4. To model the subtraction problem $(-6) - (-3)$, put six −1 chips on your table. Then take away three −1 chips.

   Complete: Since there are _____ −1 chips left,

   $(-6) - (-3) =$ _____ .

5. Explain how to use integer chips to represent $7 - 4$ and then find the difference. _____

   _____

   _____

   _____

6. To model $-3 - 5$, put down three −1 chips on the table to represent −3. You need to take away five 1 chips. But there are no 1 chips!

   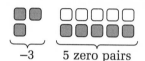

   Here is a strategy you can use. Put down five zero pairs. This does not change the value of the chips on the table, since the zero pairs have a total value of 0.

   Now remove the five 1 chips.

   What chips are left? _____

   This shows that $-3 - 5 =$ _____ .

7. Complete the integer chip diagrams to represent $4 - 6$ and $4 - (-2)$.

   $4 - 6 =$ _____ $4 - (-2) =$ _____

8. To model $3(-4)$, arrange three groups of −4.

   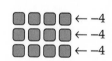

   Since the total value of the chips is _____ ,

   $3(-4) =$ _____ .

(continued)

Additional Exploration 2 *(continued)*

9. To model 15 ÷ 3 with integer chips, divide fifteen
1 chips into three equal groups. Explain how the model
shows the value of 15 ÷ 3._____

_____

_____

10. Draw integer chip diagrams to represent 5(−1) and −8 ÷ 2.

5(−1) = _____   −8 ÷ 2 = _____

Additional Exploration 3

For use with Section 2-7

How can you use algebra tiles to solve equations?

Materials: *Algebra tiles*

● ●

1. Use your algebra tiles to model the equation $2x - 1 = 5$, as shown.

2. Begin solving the equation by getting the *x*-tiles alone on one side of the equation. You can eliminate the –1-tile by adding a 1-tile to *both* sides of the equation. The 1-tile and the –1-tile are a *zero pair* because their combined value is zero. Remove the pair.

   What equation does your model now represent?

   _____

3. Since there are *two x*-tiles, rearrange the 1-tiles to form two equal rows.

   By looking at one row, you can see that each *x*-tile is

   equal to _____ .

4. Show that substituting 3 for *x* makes the equation $2x - 1 = 5$ a true statement. _____

   _____

(continued)

Name _____ Date _____

Additional Exploration 3 (continued)

5. Use your algebra tiles to copy the model shown.
    What equation does the model represent?

    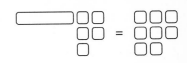

    _____

    Use the model to solve the equation.
    (*Hint:* What can you do to *both* sides to get the
    x-tile alone?)

    By looking at one row, you can see that each *x*-tile is

    equal to _____ .

6. Explain how to solve the equation $5x = -15$ by using

    algebra tiles. _____

    _____

    _____

    _____

7. The diagrams below show the steps for solving the
    equation $3x + 4 = 1$ using algebra tiles. Copy the steps
    with your tiles. Use the lines at the right to describe what
    has happened at each step.

    Step 1    _____

                                             _____

    Step 2    _____

                                             _____

    Step 3 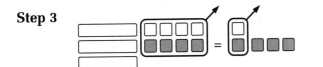   _____

                                             _____

    Step 4   _____

                                             _____

    Step 5   _____

                                             _____

(continued)

Additional Exploration 3 (continued)

Use your algebra tiles to copy each model and solve the equation it represents.

8. ⬜⬜⭕⭕⭕⭕ = ⭕⭕⭕⭕

Equation represented: _____

Solution: x = _____

9. ⬜⬜ ⬜⬜ ■■■ = ⬜⬜
⬜⬜ ⬜⬜ ■■■ = ⬜

Equation represented: _____

Solution: x = _____

10. Draw a tile diagram to represent $3x + 2 = 11$. Use your

algebra tiles to solve the equation. x = _____

Additional Exploration 4

For use with Sections 2-7 and 2-8

How can you use tables to solve problems?

Materials: *Calculator*

• •

Many problems can be solved by using equations. Another useful way to solve problems is by using tables.

1. To prepare for a book report, Alex has read 13 chapters of a 22-chapter novel. If he reads 2 chapters a day, how many more days will he need to finish the novel?
Continue filling in the table until the total number of chapters is 22 or just over 22.

Number of days	Number of Chapters $(13 + 2 \cdot \text{number of days})$
1	$13 + 2 \cdot 1 = 15$

How many chapters are added at each step of the table?

How many days will it take Alex to finish the novel?

2. Make a table to solve the following problem. Theresa has already made 24 favors for a children's holiday party. She can make 5 favors an hour, and she expects 50 children at the party. How many more hours will Theresa have

to work? _____

(continued)

Name _____ Date _____

Additional Exploration 4 *(continued)*

3. You do not always have to complete every row of a table.
Once the pattern of the table is established, you can use
three dots to indicate that rows are being skipped. Here is
a sample.
Anika wants to save $550 for a trip to Mexico. She has
$210 in the bank now and can save $15 per week from her
part-time job. How many weeks will it take her to save the
money? Use a calculator to complete the following table.

Number of Weeks	Amount Saved ($) (210 + 15 · number of weeks)
1	
2	
⋮	⋮
20	210 + 15 · 20 = __?__
21	
22	
23	

Why is 20 weeks a good place
to resume the table? _____
_____
_____
_____

How long will it take Anika to
save the money? _____

4. The Drama Club has spent $520 on expenses for its
musical production. They received $200 from the student
council and plan to sell tickets at $6 each. How many

tickets must they sell to cover expenses? _____

Guess a value.

Guess again.

Solve by guessing

and checking.

Number of Tickets	Income ($)	
20	200 + 20(6) = 320	← too low
60	200 + 60(6) = 560	← too high

5. Make a table to solve the following problem. Miguel
bought a tie and a sweatshirt for $34 altogether. He
spent three times as much for the sweatshirt as for
the tie.

What did the sweatshirt cost?

Name _____ Date _____

Additional Exploration 5

For use with Sections 5-1 and 5-3

How can you use a graphics calculator to
model situations and solve problems?

Materials: *Graphics calculator*

● ●

Note: If you have questions about operating your graphics
calculator, you can refer to the Technology Handbook or to the
instruction manual for your calculator.

**A tank contains 10 gallons of water. Every minute, 2.5 more
gallons are added. How many minutes are needed for the tank to
contain 30 gallons?**

1. An equation that models this situation is: $y = 10 + 2.5x$.
    Explain what each number and variable in the equation
    means in terms of the situation.

    10: _____

    2.5: _____

    x: _____

    y: _____

2. Enter the equation $y = 10 + 2.5x$ in your graphics
    calculator. For the viewing window, use Xmin = 0,
    Xmax = 12, Ymin = 0, and Ymax = 40. Press ⌈TRACE⌉
    and move the cursor along the graph. Get as close as you
    can to the point at which $y = 30$. Watch the coordinate
    read-out at the bottom of the screen. To get even closer,
    use the ⌈ZOOM⌉ key. After you zoom in, use ⌈TRACE⌉ once
    again. You can do this repeatedly if you wish. It appears
    that y will be equal to 30 when x is about_____ .

3. Check your solution from step 2 by substituting in the
    equation $y = 10 + 2.5x$._____

4. The tank will contain 30 gallons of water in
    _____ more minutes.

(continued)

Additional Exploration 5 *(continued)*

Suppose that some chairs were purchased for Marian Anderson
Middle School. A third of them were assigned to the new
cafeteria. These chairs along with 20 chairs that were previously
assigned to the cafeteria gave the cafeteria a total of 150 chairs.
How many chairs were purchased?

5. Explain why the equation $\frac{x}{3} + 20 = 150$ models the

    situation. _____

    _____

    _____

    _____

You can use a graphics calculator to solve an equation such as
$150 = \frac{x}{3} + 20$. Asking what number is the solution of this
equation is like asking what number will make y equal to 150
when $y = \frac{x}{3} + 20$.

6. Enter and graph the equation $y = \frac{x}{3} + 20$ on your
    calculator. Chances are you see none or almost none of the
    graph. Experiment with different viewing windows until
    you find an appropriate one. (*Hint:* You will need y-values
    greater than 150 because the problem asks you to find the
    value of x when $y = 150$.) When you've found an
    appropriate window, describe the viewing window that

    you used. _____ _____

    _____

7. Use ⎡TRACE⎤ and ⎡ZOOM⎤ to get close to the point where
    $y = 150$. At that point, to two decimal places,

    $x \approx$ _____ .

8. How do you know that you have found the value of x to

    the nearest hundredth? _____

    _____

9. Solve the equation $\frac{x}{3} + 20 = 150$ using algebra. Does the

    solution agree with the one you found using the

    calculator? _____

    _____

    (continued)

Additional Exploration 5 *(continued)*

10. What does the solution mean in terms of the situation?

_____

One student bought 5 pencils at the school store. Another student bought 8 pencils and paid 90¢ more than the first student.

11. Write an equation that models the situation. Use x to represent the cost of each pencil.

_____

12. Choose an appropriate viewing window. Then graph y = left side of the equation and y = right side of the equation. Use the trace feature to find the coordinates of the intersection point. _____

13. Use your answer from step 12 to find the cost of each pencil. _____

Additional Exploration 6

For use with Section 5-3

How can you use algebra tiles to solve equations with variables on both sides?

Materials: *Algebra tiles*

• •

Copy this model with your algebra tiles.

1. What equation does it represent?

   _____

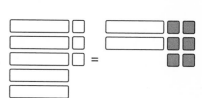

2. To solve the equation, you need to get the *x*-tiles by themselves on one side of the equals sign. First, take away two *x*-tiles from *both* sides of the model.

   Are all of the *x*-tiles on the same side now?

   _____

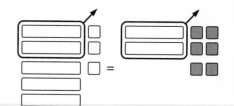

3. Next, add three −1-tiles to *both* sides of the model. After you do this, the left side of the model has three zero pairs. Remove these pairs from the model since they equal zero.

   What equation does the model now represent?

   _____

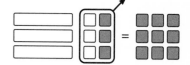

4. Since there are three *x*-tiles left, arrange each side of the model into three *equal rows.* Look at one of the rows to determine the value of one *x*-tile.

   You will find that *x* = _____ .

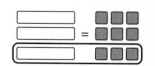

5. You know that your solution is correct because when you substitute this value for *x* in the original equation, both

   sides have a value of _____ .

(continued)

Explorations Lab Manual, INTEGRATED MATHEMATICS 1

Name _____ Date _____

Additional Exploration 6 *(continued)*

The diagrams show the steps for solving the equation
$3x - 1 = -2x - 11$ with algebra tiles. Copy the steps with your
tiles. Use the lines at the right to describe in words what has
happened at each step.

6.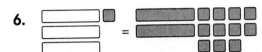
  _____

  _____

7.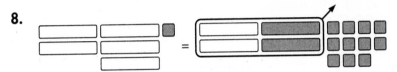
  _____

  _____

8.
  _____

  _____

9.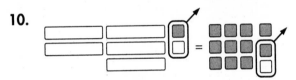
  _____

  _____

10.
  _____

  _____

11.
  _____

  _____

12.
  _____

  _____

13. What is the solution to the equation $3x - 1 = -2x - 11$?

_____

14. Check by substituting into the equation. _____

_____

15. Use algebra tiles to model the solution of the equation
$3 - 2x = 4x - 9$. (*Hint:* $3 - 2x = 3 + (-2x)$)

$x =$ _____

Name _____ Date _____

Additional Exploration 7

For use with Section 6-6

━━━━━━━━━━

How can you use geometry software to study dilations?

━━━━━━━━━━

Materials: *Computer, geometry graphing software, calculator*

• •

Plot the points $A(-3, -4)$, $B(2, -5)$, $C(5, 2)$, $D(0, 3)$, and $E(0, -2)$. Construct quadrilateral $ABCD$.

1. Transform $ABCD$ by using a dilation with center E and scale factor 0.75. (Remember to zoom in if you need to see greater detail.) Find the coordinates of the vertices of $FGHI$, the image of $ABCD$.

   $F(\_\_\_\_ , \_\_\_\_)$ $G(\_\_\_\_ , \_\_\_\_)$

   $H(\_\_\_\_ , \_\_\_\_)$ $I(\_\_\_\_ , \_\_\_\_)$

2. Construct lines $\overleftrightarrow{AF}$, $\overleftrightarrow{BG}$, $\overleftrightarrow{CH}$, and $\overleftrightarrow{DI}$. At what point do they meet? _____

3. Use *Measure* to find the lengths of corresponding sides (for example, $\overline{AB}$ and $\overline{FG}$). Use your calculator to find the ratio of the length of each image side to the length of the corresponding side in the original figure. What do you find? _____

   _____

4. Use *Measure* to compare the measure of the corresponding angles. What do you find? _____

   _____

   _____

Plot the points $A(-6, 8)$, $B(10, 3)$, $C(4, 2)$, $D(-3, -2.5)$, $E(1, -3.75)$, and $F(-0.5, -4)$. Construct $\triangle ABC$ and $\triangle DEF$. $\triangle DEF$ is the image of $\triangle ABC$ under a dilation.

5. By constructing lines through corresponding points, find the center of the dilation.

   _____

(continued)

Name _____ Date _____

Additional Exploration 7 *(continued)*

6. By using *Measure* and calculating the ratio of the lengths of the corresponding sides, find the scale factor.

_____

Experiment with figures of your own choosing to find out what happens under each set of conditions. Describe your conclusions.

7. The center of dilation is a vertex of the figure and the scale factor is between 0 and 1.

_____

_____

8. The center of dilation is inside the figure and the scale factor is greater than 1.

_____

_____

9. The center of dilation is on one of the sides of the figure and the scale factor is greater than 1.

_____

_____

10. The scale factor is 1.

_____

_____

11. The center of dilation is the origin and the scale factor is 2.

_____

_____

12. Plot the points $A(-4, -2)$, $B(8, -2)$, and $C(-4, 4)$. Then construct this design using only dilations. List the steps you used.

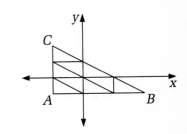

Additional Exploration 8

For use with Section 8-5

How can you use a graphics calculator to solve systems of equations?

Materials: *Graphics calculator*

● ●

Note: If you have questions about operating your graphics calculator, refer to the Technology Handbook or to the instruction manual for your calculator.

1. Use the standard settings for the viewing window. Enter the equations of the following system.

   $y = 3x + 2$

   $y = -x + 6$

   Press ⎡GRAPH⎤ to see the graphs. Use ⎡TRACE⎤ and ⎡ZOOM⎤ to estimate the coordinates of the point where the lines meet. You may not hit the point exactly with the cursor, but you can get close. Write what you think the coordinates are.

   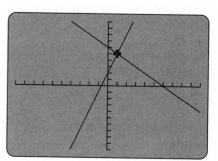

   $x =$ _____ , $y =$ _____

   Check whether these coordinates satisfy the equation.

   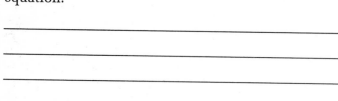

   _____

   _____

   _____

   _____

(continued)

Name _____ Date _____

Additional Exploration 8 *(continued)*

2. Again set the calculator for the standard viewing window. Clear the equations list and enter the following system.

    $y = 4x - 50$

    $y = \frac{2}{3}x + 40$

    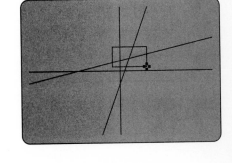

    Note that for the second equation you should enter $y = (2/3)x + 40$ or $y = 2 * x/3 + 40$. Do you see why?

    Press ⬚GRAPH⬚. The lines are outside the viewing window.

    Use ⬚ZOOM⬚ out to enlarge the viewing window until you see both lines and where they cross. Then use ⬚TRACE⬚ and ⬚ZOOM⬚ to locate the coordinates of the point of intersection.
    Write the coordinates of the point of intersection.

    $x =$ _____ , $y =$ _____

    Substitute in both equations of the system to check.

    _____

    _____

    _____

    _____

3. Many graphics calculators have a BOX feature that allows you to enlarge a rectangular area of a graph. If your calculator has this feature, redo Exercise 2 using BOX instead of tracing and zooming in.

    Which method seems easier? _____

    _____

    _____

(continued)

Name _____ Date _____

Additional Exploration 8 *(continued)*

Use your graphics calculator to solve these systems of equations.
Your answers should be correct to one decimal place. Note that
in step 6 you must solve each equation for *y* so that you can enter
the equations.

4. $y = -3.5x + 2.9$ **5.** $y = 100 - 15x$ **6.** $3x + 2y = 80$
  $y = 1.6x - 4.3$ $y = 0.11x - 20$ $4x - y = 23$

  $x =$ _____ $x =$ _____ $x =$ _____

  $y =$ _____ $y =$ _____ $y =$ _____

7. Did you know that you can use a graphics calculator to
  solve a single equation that has the variable on both sides
  of the equals sign? Suppose you want to solve

$$9 + 2(x - 11) = 32 - 3x.$$

  Set each side of the equation equal to *y*. This gives a
  system of equations.

  $y = 9 + 2(x - 11)$

  $y = 32 - 3x$

  Use your graphics calculator to find where the graphs
  intersect. When you have located the point of intersection
  or are very close to it, write what you think the actual

  x-coordinate of the point is: $x =$ _____ .

  How can you check your answer?

  _____

  _____

  _____

  _____

8. Use the method of step 7 to solve the equation
  $0.2(x - 3) = -0.28x + 18.$

  _____

Additional Exploration 9

For use with Section 9-5

How can you use models to investigate
surface areas of prisms, pyramids,
and cones?

Materials: *Oaktag or cardboard, ruler, scissors, compass, protractor,*
transparent tape or glue, calculator

• •

**Make and cut out full-size versions of these patterns using oaktag
or cardboard. Use the dimensions shown, all of which are in
inches. Cut along solid lines. Then fold and fasten along dotted
lines. Keep one base easy to open. Shaded sections are flaps.**

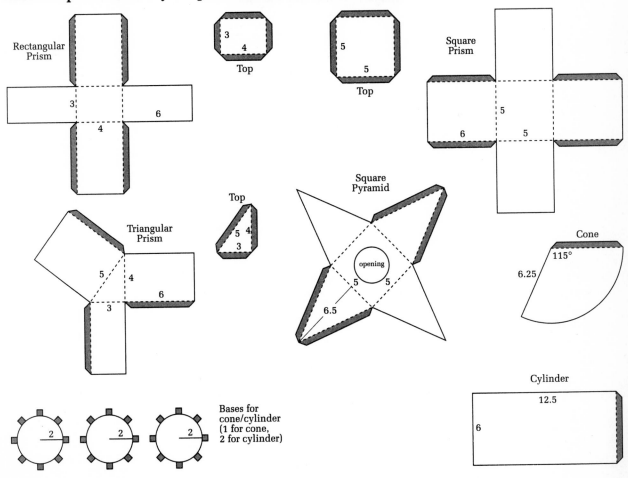

(continued)

Name _____ Date _____

Additional Exploration 9 *(continued)*

Place your assembled three-dimensional models nearby so you can refer to them. Also, place the first page of this Additional Exploration worksheet nearby. Refer to it as needed for dimensions of your models.

1. Complete the following table.

Solid	Number of bases	Total area of bases (in.^{2})	Total area of faces (in.^{2})	Total surface area (in.^{2})
Square prism				
Rectangular prism				
Triangular prism				
Square pyramid				

2. Describe how you can find the total surface area of the cylinder. What is the total surface area of your model

   cylinder? _____

   _____

   _____

   _____

   _____

3. Describe how you can find the area of the curved surface of the cone. What is the area of the curved surface of your

   model cone? _____

   _____

   _____

   _____

4. How can you find the area of the base of the cone?

   What is this area? _____

   _____

   _____

5. What is the total surface area of your model cone?

   _____

Save all your models for Additional Exploration 10.

Name _____ Date _____

Additional Exploration 10

For use with Section 9-7

How can you use models to investigate volumes of pyramids and cones?

Materials: *Models from Additional Exploration 9, rice or sand*

• •

Use your models from Additional Exploration 9.
Your square pyramid and square prism have the same height and base. Carefully pull open the bottom of the pyramid and the top of the prism. Fill the pyramid to the brim with rice or sand and pour it into the prism.

1. How many times can you fill the prism using the pyramid

    until the prism is full? _____

2. What is the ratio of the volume of the pyramid to the

    volume of the prism? _____

Repeat the experiment above using the cylinder and the cone. Note that these space figures have the same height and the same base.

3. How many times can you fill the cylinder using the cone

    until the cylinder is full? _____

4. What is the ratio of the volume of the cone to the volume

    of the cylinder? _____

5. If you weighed a cone full of rice and a cylinder full of rice
    (using your model cone and cylinder), how would their
    weights compare? Explain your thinking.

    _____

    _____

    _____

    _____

    _____

Name _____   Date _____

Additional Exploration 11

For use with Section 10-1

How can you use geometry software to investigate reflections?

Materials: *Computer, geometry software*

• •

Plot the points $A(2, 1)$, $B(4, 3)$, $C(5, 2)$, $D(6, 3)$, $E(4, 5)$, and $F(1, 2)$ on your screen. Construct $ABCDEF$.

1. Reflect the "L" shape over the y-axis. Sketch the result on the grid at the right.

2. Reflect the original "L" shape over the x-axis. Sketch the result at the right.

3. Complete the design in the third quadrant by reflecting one of the "L" shapes over one of the axes. Sketch the result on the same grid. How did

    you do it? _____

    _____

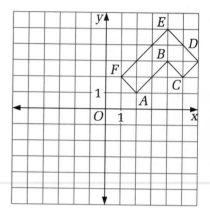

4. Clear the screen and redraw the original "L" shape. Draw the line $y = x$ and reflect the "L" shape over

    the line. What is the result? _____

    _____

5. Clear the screen and redraw the original "L" shape. What will be the result if the shape is reflected over

    line AF? _____

    Sketch your prediction on the graph at the right. Check your prediction using geometry software.

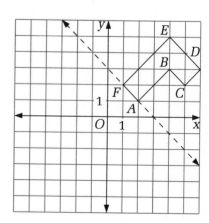

Clear your screen. Then plot the points $A(0, 0)$, $B(-3, 4)$, and $C(4, 3)$. Construct $\triangle ABC$. Graph the line $y = 0.5x - 3$ (Line 1). Reflect $\triangle ABC$ over Line 1.

6. The images of A, B, and C are $D($ _____ , _____ $)$

    $E($ _____ , _____ $)$, and $F($ _____ , _____ $)$

(continued)

Additional Exploration 11 *(continued)*

7. Use *Measure* to compare the lengths of corresponding sides. What do you find?

_____

_____

8. Use *Measure* to compare the measures of corresponding

angles. What do you find? _____

_____

9. Draw line *AD*. Construct point *G* where $\overleftrightarrow{AD}$ intersects

Line 1. The coordinates of *G* are (_____ , _____).
Use *Measure* to complete the following:

$AG =$ _____ and $DG =$ _____ .

10. Draw line *BE*. Construct point *H* where $\overleftrightarrow{BE}$ intersects

Line 1. The coordinates of *H* are (_____ , _____).
Use *Measure* to complete the following:

$BH =$ _____ and $EH =$ _____ .

11. Draw line *CF*. Construct point *I* where $\overleftrightarrow{CF}$ intersects

Line 1. The coordinates of *I* are (_____ , _____).
Use *Measure* to complete the following:

$CI =$ _____ and $FI =$ _____ .

12. What pattern do you recognize in the answers to steps 9–11?

_____

_____

13. Now use the software to find equations of $\overleftrightarrow{AD}$, $\overleftrightarrow{BE}$, and $\overleftrightarrow{CF}$. What do you notice about the equations?

_____

_____

14. Steps 6–13 demonstrate that for a reflection, the

reflection line is always _____

to and divides in half the segment connecting a point and its image.

(continued)

Explorations Lab Manual, INTEGRATED MATHEMATICS 1

25

Additional Exploration 11 *(continued)*

Use the idea from step 14 to help with steps 15–18.
Construct △*ABC* and △*DEF* and decide whether or not △*DEF* is
the image of △*ABC* for a reflection. If it is, write the equation of
the line of reflection. If it is not, write *not a reflection*.

15. $A(0, 0)$, $B(3, 9)$, $C(6, 0)$, $D(6, -6)$, $E(15, -3)$, $F(6, 0)$

_____

16. $A(0, 2)$, $B(2, 0)$, $C(3, 3)$, $D(-3, 2)$, $E(-1, 0)$, $F(0, 3)$

_____

17. $A(4.8, -0.4)$, $B(10.4, -1.2)$, $C(0, 6)$, $D(-4, 4)$, $E(-8, -8)$,

$F(4, 4)$ _____

18. $A(2, 5)$, $B(4, -2)$, $C(-2, -3)$, $D(-8, -5)$, $E(-1, -7)$, $F(0, -1)$

_____

19. Plot the points $A(6, 1)$, $B(8, 3)$, and $C(0, 0)$. Construct
△*ABC*. Then use only reflections to create this design.

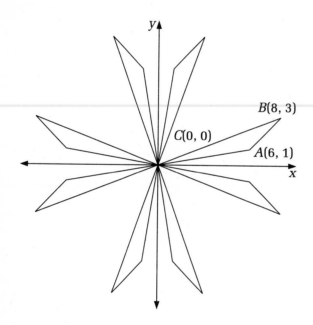

Name _____   Date _____

Additional Exploration 12

This Exploration may be substituted for the Exploration in the text.

For use with Section 10-2

How can you find other functions whose graphs are parabolas?

Materials: *Tracing paper*

• •

1. Trace this graph of $y = x^2$ on tracing paper. (Do not trace the axes.) What is the name for this kind of curve?

   _____

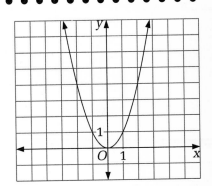

2. Complete this table of values for the function $y = x^2 + 4$.

x	$y = x^2 + 4$
−2	
−1	
0	
1	
2	

   Plot the five points on the graph at the right. Connect the points with a curve.

3. Place your tracing on the graph. Slide your tracing to translate the graph of $y = x^2$ up 4 units.
   Look at the tracing and at the graph. Are the five points you plotted for the function $y = x^2 + 4$ also on the

   translated graph of $y = x^2$? _____

4. If you graphed $y = x^2 - 4$, would your tracing fit exactly over the graph? Explain your thinking.

   _____

   _____

   _____

   _____

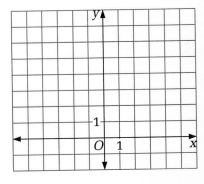

(continued)

Additional Exploration 12 *(continued)*

5. Complete the table and draw the graph for $y = (x - 4)^2$.
Then slide your tracing to translate the graph of $y = x^2$ to
the *right* 4 units. What do you notice?

$y = (x - 4)^2$	
x	**y**
2	
3	
4	
5	
6	

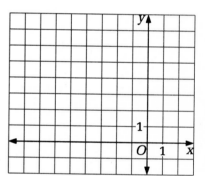

6. Complete the table and draw the graph for $y = (x + 4)^2$.
Then slide your tracing to translate the graph of $y = x^2$ to
the *left* 4 units. What do you notice?

$y = (x + 4)^2$	
x	**y**
−6	
−5	
−4	
−3	
−2	

Summarize your findings by answering these questions.

7. How is the graph of $y = x^2$ shifted when a positive number is
added to or subtracted from x^2?

_____

_____

8. How is the graph of $y = x^2$ shifted when a positive number is
added to or subtracted from x *before* squaring?

_____

_____

Name _____ Date _____

Additional Exploration 13

For use with Section 10-6

━━━━━━━━━━

How can you use algebra tiles to multiply binomials?

Materials: *Algebra tiles*

● ●

1. Suppose your algebra tiles have the dimensions shown below. Write the area of each tile in the blank below the tile.

Area = _____   Area = _____   Area = _____

Step 1   **Step 2**

2. Add the areas of the tiles to find the area of the square at the right above.

Area = (_____)² = _____ + _____ + _____

3. Use your algebra tiles to copy the model at the right. Use 1-tiles to complete the rectangle with no overlapping tiles.

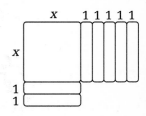

How many 1-tiles did you use? _____

Adding the areas of the tiles shows that the area of the

rectangle is _____ + _____ + _____.

4. The area of a rectangle is length · width, so the area of the

rectangle in step 3 is (x + 5) · _____ .

The model shows that Area = _____ · _____ =

_____ + _____ + _____.

5. Use the distributive property to multiply (x + 4)(x + 2).

(x + 4)(x + 2) =

(x + 4) · _____ + (x + 4) · _____ =

_____ + _____ + _____ + _____

(continued)

Additional Exploration 13 *(continued)*

6. Use algebra tiles to model $(x + 4)(x + 2)$.
Look at your model and find the regions that match each of
the four terms of the multiplication in step 5. When you
combine like terms, you get
$$(x + 4)(x + 2) = x^2 + 6x + 8.$$
Where does $6x$ come from on your model?

_____

_____

7. Use algebra tiles to copy the model at the right.
Fill it in with x-tiles and 1-tiles to form a
rectangle. How many x-tiles did you use?_____

How many 1-tiles? _____ The model shows
that Area $= (2x + 3) \cdot (x + 1) =$

_____ + _____ + _____ .

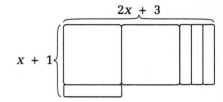

$2x + 3$

$x + 1$

8. Now multiply $(2x + 3)(x + 1)$ using the
distributive property.

$(2x + 3)(x + 1) =$

$(2x + 3) \cdot$ _____ $+ (2x + 3) \cdot$ _____ $=$

_____ + _____ + _____ + _____ $=$

_____ + _____ + _____

Combine like terms. Look at your model from step 7.
Notice which region corresponds to each term of
the product.

9. The figure at the right models

_____ $\cdot$ _____ .

Area A is $3x \cdot x$, or $3x^2$.

Area B is $x \cdot 2$, or _____ .

Area C is _____ $\cdot$ _____ , or _____ .

Area D is _____ $\cdot$ _____ , or _____ .

The product $(3x + 2)(x + 4)$ equals
A + B + C + D, or

_____ + _____ + _____ + _____ $=$

_____ + _____ + _____ .

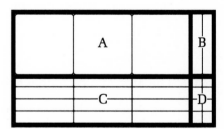

(continued)

Additional Exploration 13 *(continued)*

Use algebra tiles to find each product.

10. $(x + 3)(x + 3) =$ _____

11. $(2x + 1)(x + 3) =$ _____

12. $(5x + 2)(2x + 3) =$ _____

Summarize your findings.

13. If you wanted to use algebra tiles to model

    $(4x + 7)(x + 3)$, you would need _____ x^2-tiles,

    _____ x-tiles, and _____ 1-tiles. This tells you

    that $(4x + 7)(x + 3) =$

    _____ .

14. If you wanted to use algebra tiles to model

    $(3x + 2)(4x + 5)$, you would need _____ x^2-tiles,

    _____ x-tiles, and _____1-tiles. This tells you that

    $(3x + 2)(4x + 5) =$ _____ .

Additional Exploration 14

For use with Section 10-7

─────────

How can you use algebra tiles to factor trinomials?

─────────

Materials: *Algebra tiles*

● ●

1. Start with the algebra tiles shown at the right.

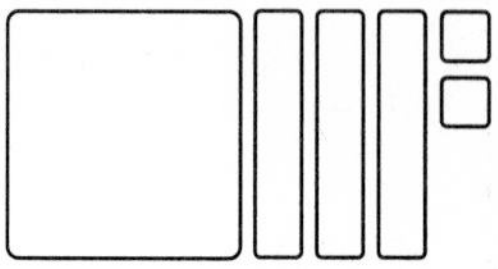

    What expression do they represent? _____

    Use the tiles to build a rectangle.

    What is the length of the rectangle? _____

    What is the width? _____

    Complete this statement:

    Area of Rectangle = length • width =

    _____ • _____ =

    _____ + _____ + _____ .

    The expression $(x + 2)(x + 1)$ is the **factored form** of the trinomial $x^2 + 3x + 2$. The algebra tiles show that the two expressions are equal because each can be represented using the same set of algebra tiles.

2. Use tiles representing the trinomial $x^2 + 7x + 10$ to build a rectangle.

    What tiles do you need? _____

    _____

    What is the length of the rectangle you built? _____

    What is the width? _____

    What is $x^2 + 7x + 10$ in factored form?

    (_____)(_____)

    Check your answer by expanding the factored form.

(continued)

Additional Exploration 14 *(continued)*

3. Take out algebra tiles representing $x^2 + 11x + 24$. Suppose you want to build a rectangle with these tiles. Which arrangement of the x^2-tile and the 24 1-tiles will allow you

   to form a rectangle with the 11 x-tiles? _____

   a.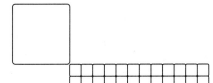

   b.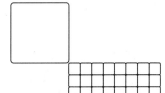

   c.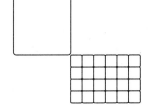

4. Which arrangement shown in step 3 would allow you

   to model $x^2 + 14x + 24$?_____

5. Which arrangement shown in step 3 would allow you

   to model $x^2 + 10x + 24$?_____

6. Fill in this table about steps 3–5.

Trinomial Expression	Middle Term	Arrangement of 1-tiles
$x^2 + 11x + 24$	11x	Rectangle: length 8, width 3
$x^2 + 14x + 24$		
$x^2 + 10x + 24$		

7. What pattern does the table for step 6 suggest?

   _____

   _____

8. Use algebra tiles to factor $x^2 + 8x + 15$. The 1-tiles are

   arranged in a rectangle with length _____ and

   width _____. How do these dimensions relate to

   the middle term $8x$? _____

   _____

   In factored form, $x^2 + 8x + 15 = ($ _____ $)($ _____ $)$.

(continued)

Additional Exploration 14 *(continued)*

9. Use algebra tiles to factor $x^2 + 10x + 21$. The 1-tiles are arranged in a rectangle with length _____ and width

   _____. How do these dimensions relate to the

   middle term $10x$? _____

   _____

   In factored form, $x^2 + 10x + 21 =$

   (_____)(_____).

10. Use algebra tiles to try to factor $x^2 + 10x + 8$. How many different arrangements of the eight 1-tiles are there?

    _____

    Why don't any of them work? _____

    _____

    _____

    _____

11. Summarize the process of factoring a trinomial $x^2 + bx + c$ with algebra tiles. Be sure to explain how the factors relate to the numbers b and c._____

    _____

    _____

    _____

Diagram Master 1

Geoboards

Diagram Master 2

Graph Paper

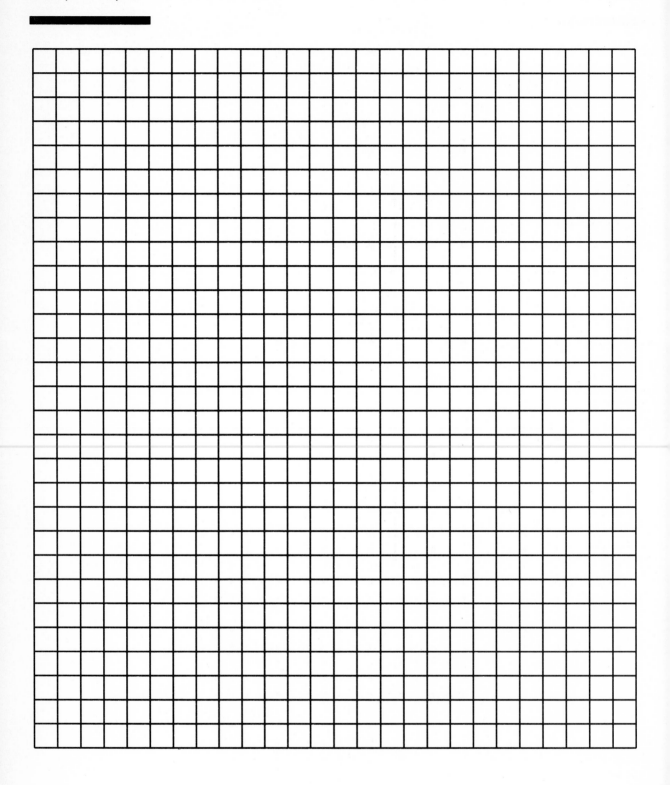

Diagram Master 3

Coordinate Grids

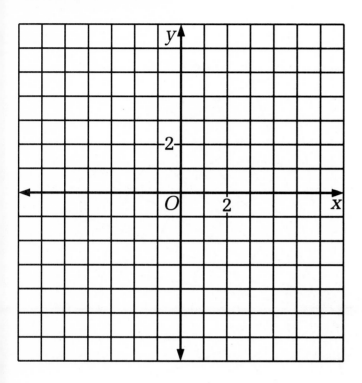

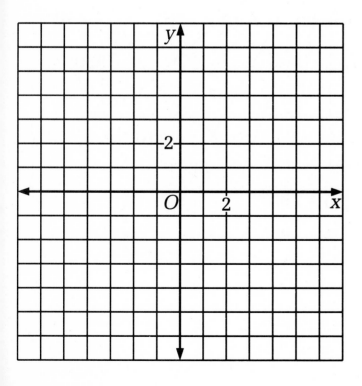

Diagram Master 4

Polar Graph Paper

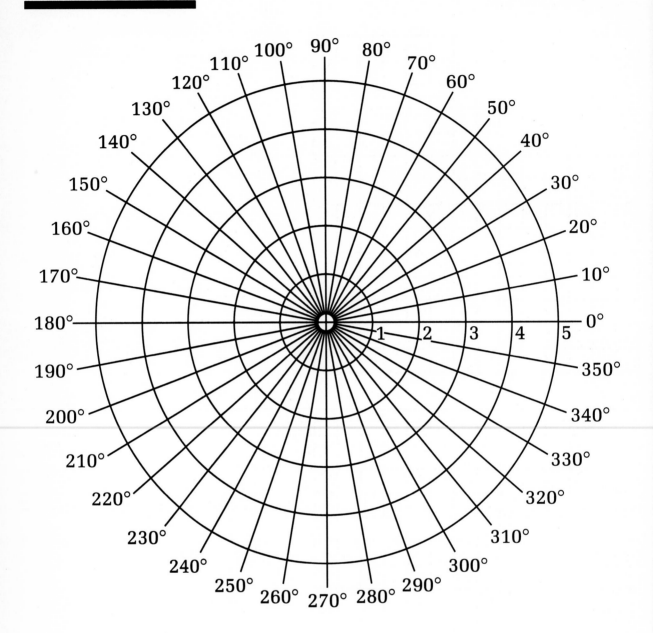

Diagram Master 5

Integer Chips

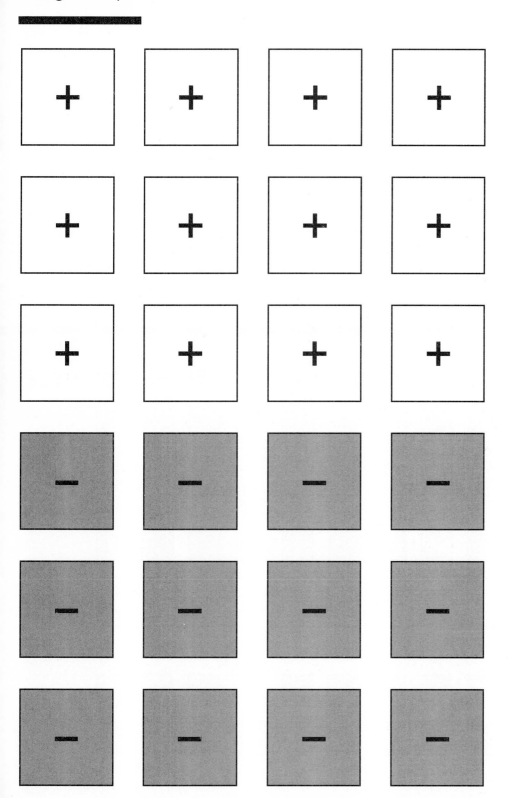

Diagram Master 6

Algebra Tiles

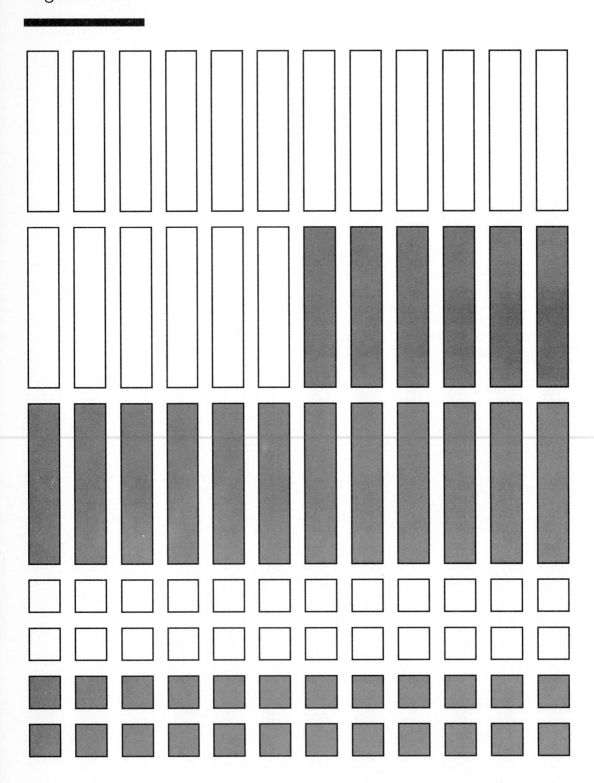

Diagram Master 7

Algebra Tiles

Diagram Master 8

For use with Section 1-2 Exploration

Number of x-tiles	Perimeter	
	Long Rectangles	Tall Rectangles
1		
2		
3		
4		
5		
6		
7		
8		
9		
10		

Number of x-tiles	Perimeter	
	Long Rectangles	Tall Rectangles
1		
2		
3		
4		
5		
6		
7		
8		
9		
10		

Diagram Master 9

For use with Section 1-6 Explorations

Diagram Master 10

For use with Section 2-3 Exploration

power	decimal	fraction
10^4	10,000	—
10^3		—
10^2		—
10^1		—
10^0		—
10^{-1}	0.1	$\frac{1}{10}$
10^{-2}		
10^{-3}		

power	decimal	fraction
10^4	10,000	—
10^3		—
10^2		—
10^1		—
10^0		—
10^{-1}	0.1	$\frac{1}{10}$
10^{-2}		
10^{-3}		

Diagram Master 11

For use with Section 3-1 Exploration

Which types of volunteer work most interest you? Please rank types of volunteer work in order. Write "1" next to your first choice, "2" next to your second choice, and so on. Feel free to put in your own choices in the selections marked "other," if you don't see them already listed.

Hospital _____

Work with elderly _____

Big sister/big brother _____

Homeless shelter _____

Tutoring _____

Recycling _____

Animal shelter _____

other _____

other _____

other _____

other _____

other _____

other _____

Which types of volunteer work most interest you? Please rank types of volunteer work in order. Write "1" next to your first choice, "2" next to your second choice, and so on. Feel free to put in your own choices in the selections marked "other," if you don't see them already listed.

Hospital _____

Work with elderly _____

Big sister/big brother _____

Homeless shelter _____

Tutoring _____

Recycling _____

Animal shelter _____

other _____

other _____

other _____

other _____

other _____

other _____

Diagram Master 12

For use with Section 4-5 Exploration

Name	Height (cm)	Lower-Arm Length (cm)

Name	Height (cm)	Lower-Arm Length (cm)

Explorations Lab Manual, INTEGRATED MATHEMATICS 1

Diagram Master 13

For use with Section 4-7 Exploration

Number	Square of the Number
x	
−3	
−2.5	
−2	
−1.7	
−1.3	
−1	
−0.5	
0	
0.5	
1	
1.3	
1.7	
2	
2.5	
3	

Diagram Master 14

For use with Section 6-2 Exploration

	Number of Spins	Number of Landings on Red	$\dfrac{\text{number of landings on red}}{\text{number of spins}}$
Student 1	10		$= \dfrac{}{10}$
Students 1 and 2	20		$= \dfrac{}{20}$
Students 1, 2, and 3	30		$= \dfrac{}{30}$

	Number of Spins	Number of Landings on Red	$\dfrac{\text{number of landings on red}}{\text{number of spins}}$
Student 1	10		$= \dfrac{}{10}$
Students 1 and 2	20		$= \dfrac{}{20}$
Students 1, 2, and 3	30		$= \dfrac{}{30}$

	Number of Spins	Number of Landings on Red	$\dfrac{\text{number of landings on red}}{\text{number of spins}}$
Student 1	10		$= \dfrac{}{10}$
Students 1 and 2	20		$= \dfrac{}{20}$
Students 1, 2, and 3	30		$= \dfrac{}{30}$

Explorations Lab Manual, INTEGRATED MATHEMATICS 1

Diagram Master 15

For use with Section 6-2 Exploration

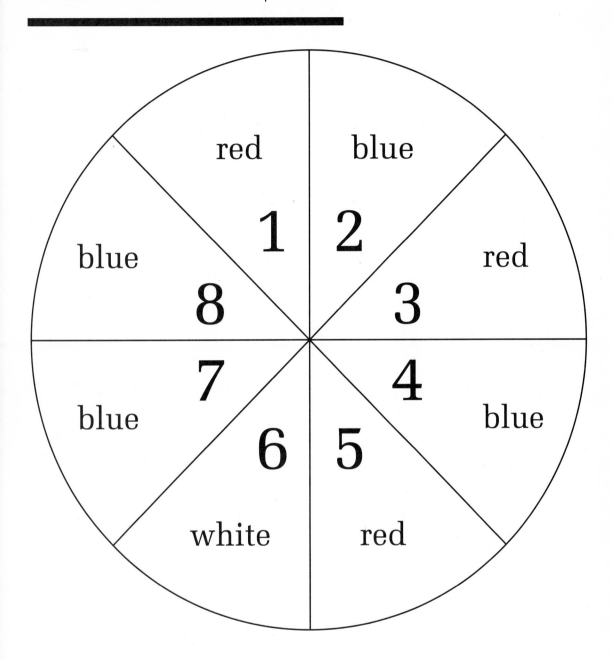

Diagram Master 16

For use with Section 6-4 Exploration

X	X	X	X	X	X	X	X	X	X
X	X	X	X	X	X	X	X	X	X

Diagram Master 17

For use with Section 6-5 Exploration

	original photograph	$\dfrac{\text{enlarged photograph}}{\text{original photograph}}$
enlarged photograph		
width		
height		

	original photograph	$\dfrac{\text{enlarged photograph}}{\text{original photograph}}$
enlarged photograph		
width		
height		

	original photograph	$\dfrac{\text{enlarged photograph}}{\text{original photograph}}$
enlarged photograph		
width		
height		

Diagram Master 18

For use with Section 6-7 Exploration

	AC	BC	AB	$\dfrac{AC}{BC}$	$\dfrac{BC}{AB}$
△1	3	4	5		
△2					
△3					
△4					

	AC	BC	AB	$\dfrac{AC}{BC}$	$\dfrac{BC}{AB}$
△1	3	4	5		
△2					
△3					
△4					

Diagram Master 19

For use with Section 7-2 Exploration

Kind of Ball:					
Drop Height, D	Bounce Heights				Mean Bounce Height, B	Ratio $\frac{B}{D}$

Kind of Ball:					
Drop Height, D	Bounce Heights				Mean Bounce Height, B	Ratio $\frac{B}{D}$

Diagram Master 20

For use with Section 7-3 Exploration

Circle	Diameter d (mm)	Circumference C (mm)	$\frac{C}{d}$
1			
2			
3			
4			
5			

Circle	Diameter d (mm)	Circumference C (mm)	$\frac{C}{d}$
1			
2			
3			
4			
5			

Diagram Master 21

For use with Section 9-1 Exploration

Triangle	Lengths of sides			Squares of lengths of sides		
	x	y	z	x^2	y^2	z^2
$\triangle A$	3	4	5	9	16	25
$\triangle B$						
$\triangle C$						
$\triangle D$						

Triangle	Lengths of sides			Squares of lengths of sides		
	x	y	z	x^2	y^2	z^2
$\triangle A$	3	4	5	9	16	25
$\triangle B$						
$\triangle C$						
$\triangle D$						

Diagram Master 22

For use with Section 9-4 Exploration

group	wins	losses	$\dfrac{\text{number of wins}}{\text{20 trials}}$
1			
2			
3			
4			
5			
6			
7			
8			
9			
10			
11			
12			
13			
14			
15			

class mean probability = $\dfrac{\text{total number of wins}}{\text{total number of trials}}$ =

Explorations Lab Manual, INTEGRATED MATHEMATICS 1

Answers

Additional Exploration 1

1. **2.**

3. 5, 7   **4.** $5x + 7$ **5.** $5x + 7$ **6.** $x^2 + 3x + 5$

7.   **8.** 3, 4, 8

9. $3x^2 + 4x + 8$ **10.** $x^2 + 3x + 5; 3x^2 + 4x + 8$

11.

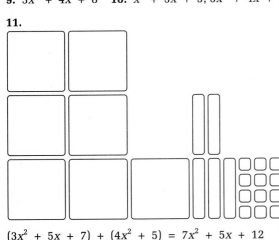

$(3x^2 + 5x + 7) + (4x^2 + 5) = 7x^2 + 5x + 12$

Additional Exploration 2

1. 3; −6; 0   **2.** 4; −4   **3.** Put down two −1 chips and six 1 chips. Remove two zero pairs. Since four 1 chips are left, $-2 + 6 = 4$.   **4.** 3; −3   **5.** Put down seven 1 chips and take away four of them. Since three 1 chips are left, $7 - 4 = 3$.   **6.** eight −1 chips; −8

7.

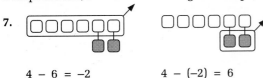

$4 - 6 = -2$ $4 - (-2) = 6$

8. −12, −12   **9.** Since there are five 1 chips in each group, $15 \div 3 = 5$.

10.

$5(-1) = -5$ $-8 \div 2 = -4$

Additional Exploration 3

1. Check students' work.   **2.** $2x = 6$ **3.** 3
4. $2(3) - 1 = 6 - 1 = 5$ **5.** $x + 5 = 8; x = 3$
6. Put out five x-tiles and fifteen −1-tiles. Arrange the

tiles on each side into five identical rows. Each row has 1 x-tile and three −1-tiles, so $x = -3$.   **7.** Step 1: The equation has been modeled using algebra tiles. Step 2: Four −1-tiles are added to each side. Step 3: Zero pairs are removed from each side. Step 4: The remaining tiles are arranged in three equal rows on each side. Step 5: The solution is found by using one row of tiles. The solution of the equation is −1.
8. $x + 4 = 4; 0$ **9.** $4x - 5 = 3; 2$

10.

Solution: 3

Additional Exploration 4

1. The table should be filled in through row five. Column 1: 1, 2, 3, 4, 5; Column 2: 15, 17, 19, 21, 23; 2 chapters; 5 days

2.

Number of Hours	Number of Favors
1	$24 + 5(1) = 29$
2	$24 + 5(2) = 34$
3	$24 + 5(3) = 39$
4	$24 + 5(4) = 44$
5	$24 + 5(5) = 49$
6	$24 + 5(6) = 54$

She must work 6 hr more.

3.

Number of Weeks	Amount Saved ($)
1	$210 + 15(1) = 225$
2	$210 + 15(2) = 240$
⋮	⋮
20	$210 + 15(20) = 510$
21	$210 + 15(21) = 525$
22	$210 + 15(22) = 540$
23	$210 + 15(23) = 555$

Since $15(20) = 300$, you can estimate mentally that $210 + 15(20)$ is close to 550. It will take Anika 23 weeks to save the money for the trip.   **4.** Check students' tables. Fifty-four tickets must be sold to cover expenses.   **5.** $25.50

Additional Exploration 5

1. 10 is the number of gallons at the start; 2.5 is the number of gallons added each minute; x is the number of minutes during which more water is added; and y

the total number of gallons when x minutes have gone by.   **2.** 8   **3.** $10 + 2.5(8) = 30$ **4.** 8
5. The total number of cafeteria chairs, 150, results from 20 previously assigned chairs and one third of the newly purchased chairs.   **6.** Answers may vary. For example, Xmin $= 0$, Xmax $= 500$, Ymin $= 0$, Ymax $= 200$.   **7.** $x \approx 390.00$.   **8.** When the value of x changes only in the thousandth place as y changes from under 150 to over 150, you can be sure the x-value is correct to two decimal places.   **9.** The solution is $x = 390$. This solution agrees with the calculator answer.
10. 390 chairs were purchased.   **11.** $5x + 90 = 8x$
12. (30, 240)   **13.** 30¢

Additional Exploration 6
1. $5x + 3 = 2x - 6$ **2.** Yes.   **3.** $3x = -9$
4. -3 **5.** -12 **6.** The equation has been modeled with algebra tiles.   **7.** Two x-tiles have been added to both sides.   **8.** Zero pairs are removed   **9.** A 1-tile has been added to both sides.   **10.** Zero pairs are removed.   **11.** The remaining tiles are arranged in five equal rows on each side.   **12.** The solution is found by using one row of tiles from each side.
13. The solution of the equation is $x = -2$.
14. $3(-2) - 1 \overset{?}{=} (-2)(-2) - 11; -7 = -7$ ✔
15. 2

Additional Exploration 7
1. $F(-2.25, -3.5)$, $G(1.5, -4.25)$, $H(3.75, 1)$, $I(0, 1.75)$
2. $(0, -2)$, or E **3.** Each ratio is 3 : 4, or 0.75.
4. Corresponding angles have the same measure.
5. $(-2, -6)$ **6.** 0.25, or $\frac{1}{4}$ **7–11.** Answers may vary. An example is given.   **7.** The image is smaller than the original and the image is contained inside the original figure.   **8.** The image is larger than the original figure and contains the original figure in its interior.   **9.** The image is larger than the original figure and the side that contains the center of dilation is contained in the image of that side.   **10.** The image is the same as the figure itself.   **11.** The coordinates of each point in the image are obtained by multiplying the coordinates of the corresponding point on the original figure by 2.   **12.** For example, construct dilations of $\triangle ABC$ with centers A, B, C and with scale factors $\frac{1}{3}$ and $\frac{2}{3}$.

Additional Exploration 8
1. 1, 5; $5 \overset{?}{=} 3(1) + 2, 5 = 5$ ✔;
$5 \overset{?}{=} -1 + 6, 5 = 5$ ✔   **2.** 27, 58; $58 \overset{?}{=} 4(27) - 50$,
$58 = 58$ ✔; $58 \overset{?}{=} \frac{2}{3}(27) + 40, 58 \overset{?}{=} 58$ ✔
3. Answers may vary.   **4.** 1.4, -2.0 **5.** 7.9, -19.1
6. 11.5, 22.8   **7.** 9; Substitute 9 for x in the original equation.   **8.** 38.75

Additional Exploration 9
1.

Solid	Number of bases	Total area of bases	Total area of faces	Total surface area
Square prism	2	50 in.^{2}	120 in.^{2}	170 in.^{2}
Rectangular prism	2	24 in.^{2}	84 in.^{2}	108 in.^{2}
Triangular prism	2	12 in.^{2}	72 in.^{2}	84 in.^{2}
Square pyramid	1	25 in.^{2}	65 in.^{2}	90 in.^{2}

2. Use $A = \pi r^2$ to find the area of one base. Double the result to get the total area of the bases. For the area of the curved surface, multiply the length and width of the rectangle that was rolled up to form the curved surface. Add the result to the total area of the bases. The total surface area of the model cylinder is about 100.1 in.^{2}.   **3.** Find the area of the circular sector used to make the curved surface. This area is about 39.2 in.^{2}.
4. Use $A = \pi r^2$ with $r = 2$. This area is about 12.6 in.^{2}.   **5.** about 51.8 in.^{2}

Additional Exploration 10
1. 3 times   **2.** 1 : 3   **3.** 3 times   **4.** 1 : 3
5. The cylinder full of rice would weigh about 3 times as much as the cone full of rice. The weights should be proportional to the volumes of the containers.

Additional Exploration 11
1–3.

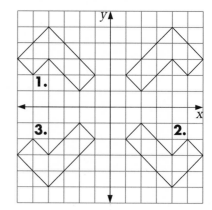

3. Answers may vary. The figure for Exercise 3 can be obtained by reflecting the figure for Exercise 1 over the x-axis or by reflecting the figure for Exercise 2 over the y-axis.   **4.** a "T" shape in the first quadrant

5.

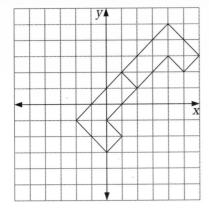

Predictions may vary. The image is a "C" shape.
6. $D(2.4, -4.8)$, $E(3.8, -9.6)$, $F(7.2, -3.4)$
7. Corresponding sides are congruent.
8. Corresponding angles are congruent.
9. $G(1.2, -2.4)$; $AG = 2.68$, $DG = 2.68$
10. $H(0.4, -2.8)$; $BH = 7.60$, $EH = 7.60$
11. $I(5.6, -0.2)$; $CI = 3.58$, $FI = 3.58$ **12.** Answers
may vary. An example is given. Line 1 intersects the
segments joining corresponding points at the
midpoints of the segments. **13.** The equations show
that the lines are all parallel and have a slope that is
the negative reciprocal of 0.5. **14.** perpendicular
15. Yes. $y = x - 6$ **16.** not a reflection **17.** not a
reflection **18.** Yes. $y = -x - 3$ **19.** Check
students' designs.

Additional Exploration 12

1. parabola **2.** 8; 5; 4; 5; 8 **3.** Yes. **4.** Yes. The
graph of $y = x^2 - 4$ would have the same shape as the
graph of $y = x^2$. The graph of $y = x^2 - 4$ is the graph
of $y = x^2$ shifted down 4 units. **5.** Table: 4; 1; 0; 1; 4;
the graph of $y = (x - 4)^2$ is the graph of $y = x^2$
shifted 4 units to the right. **6.** Table: 4; 1; 0; 1; 4; the
graph of $y = (x + 4)^2$ is the graph of $y = x^2$ shifted 4
units to the left. **7.** Adding a positive number shifts
the graph of $y = x^2$ up; subtracting a positive number
shifts the graph down. **8.** Adding a positive number
to x before squaring shifts the graph of $y = x^2$ to the
left; subtracting a positive number shifts the graph to
the right.

Additional Exploration 13

1. x^2; x; 1 **2.** Area $= (x + 1)^2 = x^2 + 2x + 1$
3. 10; $x^2 + 7x + 10$
4. $(x + 2)$; $(x + 5)(x + 2) = x^2 + 7x + 10$
5. x; 2; $x^2 + 4x + 2x + 8$ **6.** 4 x-tiles and 2 x-tiles,
or 6 x-tiles in all **7.** 1; 3; $2x^2 + 5x + 3$
8. x; 1; $2x^2 + 3x + 2x + 3 = 2x^2 + 5x + 3$
9. $(3x + 2)(x + 4)$; $2x$; $3x \cdot 4$, or $12x$; $4 \cdot 2$, or 8;
$3x^2 + 2x + 12x + 8 = 3x^2 + 14x + 8$
10. $x^2 + 6x + 9$ **11.** $2x^2 + 7x + 3$
12. $10x^2 + 19x + 6$ **13.** 4; 19; 21; $4x^2 + 19x + 21$
14. 12; 23; 10; $12x^2 + 23x + 10$

Additional Exploration 14

1. $x^2 + 3x + 2$; $x + 2$; $x + 1$; $(x + 2)(x + 1) =$
$x^2 + 3x + 2$ **2.** 1 x^2-tile, 7 x-tiles, 10 1-tiles; $x + 5$;
$x + 2$; $(x + 5)(x + 2)$ **3.** b **4.** a **5.** c **6.** $14x$,
Rectangle: length 12, width 2; $10x$, Rectangle: length 6,
width 4 **7.** Answers may vary. An example is given.
The numbers for the dimensions of the rectangle of
1-tiles must have a sum equal to the coefficient of x.
8. 5, 3; the sum of 5 and 3 is equal to the number x is
multiplied by; $(x + 5)(x + 3)$ **9.** 7, 3; the sum of
7 and 3 is equal to the number x is multiplied by;
$(x + 7)(x + 3)$ **10.** There are only two sets of
numbers: 1 by 8 and 2 by 4; neither pair of numbers
has a sum of 10. **11.** Look for a pair of numbers with
a product equal to c and a sum equal to b, say m and n.
Then form a rectangle with length $x + m$ and width
$x + n$.
